Learn about

TOOTH PARENTING

A healthly smile is always in fashion

Learn about

TOOTH PARENTING

A healthly smile is always in fashion

Dr. UNNATI GUPTA

BDS

STERLING PAPERBACKS
An imprint of
Sterling Publishers (P) Ltd.
A-59, Okhla Industrial Area, Phase-II,
New Delhi-110020. CIN: U22110PB1964PTC002569
Tel: 26387070, 26386209; Fax: 91-11-26383788
E-mail: mail@sterlingpublishers.com
www.sterlingpublishers.com

TOOTH PARENTING
A healthly smile is always in fashion
© 2015, *Dr. Unnati Gupta*
ISBN 978 81 207 9902 8

The author wishes to thank all academicians, scientists and writers who have been a source of inspiration.

The author and publisher specifically disclaim any liability, loss or risk, whatsoever, personal or otherwise, which is incurred as a consequence, directly or indirectly of the use and application of any of the contents of this book.

All rights are reserved.
No part of this publication may be reproduced, stored in a retrieval system or transmitted, in any form or by any means, mechanical, photocopying, recording or otherwise, without prior written permission of the authors.

Printed and Published by Sterling Publishers Pvt. Ltd.,
New Delhi-110020.

Dedicated to

My Loving Parents

Contents

1. Dental Care for Moms-to-Be — 7
2. From Bud to Tooth
   Eruption and Shedding of Teeth — 11
3. Hello! I Am Your Tooth
   The Chewing Apparatus — 18
4. Milk Teeth and Their Importance — 22
5. The Monster
   Dental Caries — 25
6. Eating for a Juicy Smile
   Nutrition, Diet, and Dentistry — 37
7. We Call Them Bad—Habits — 41
8. I Love to Brush!
   Routine Dental Care — 51
9. Dentist—My Best Friend!
   Regular Visits to the Dentist — 59
10. Beautiful Smile
    Orthodontics for Your Child — 65
11. More Blessed or Less
    Children with Special Needs — 75

Dental Care for Moms-to-Be

𝓔 pics have been written about a mother's love for her child. Do you know that bonding between the mother and child starts as soon as the pregnancy is confirmed? This is a very special time emotionally but also requires a lot of care. Adequate measures need to be taken to ensure a healthy and problem-free pregnancy for the mother and a sound foundation for the baby in the mother's womb.

There are a lot of myths regarding the damage to teeth during pregnancy. Women usually complain that their teeth deteriorated during pregnancy. Most of the myths develop because of lack of knowledge and inadequate dental care during this time. Some of the important but neglected aspects related to dental problems during pregnancy have been described below:

1. **Nutrition:** Nutrition is of utmost importance both for the general health as well as oral health of the mother-to-be and soon-to-be-born child. A balanced diet of chapattis, rice, fruits, vegetables, milk, cheese, yoghurt, and so on provides the

Fig. 1.1

necessary carbohydrates, proteins, vitamins, and minerals for a holistic development. The calcium present in the diet may not be sufficient, hence, should be supplemented for the development of healthy teeth and bones of the foetus and to prevent its deficiency in the mother as well.

2. **Raised hormonal levels:** Due to changes in the hormone levels in the body of the expectant mother, there may be swelling and bleeding from her gums. Sometimes, due to the abnormally high levels of hormones, there can be an exaggerated response to the tartar that has deposited around the teeth, but this can be controlled by professional cleaning by a dentist, which is technically called "scaling". The swelling of the gums usually subsides once the baby is born. Another problem that can be seen is a tumour-like growth on the gums. This is called "pregnancy tumour". This, again, regresses once the baby is born and the hormonal levels come within the normal limits. A visit to the dentist is advised during the first and second trimesters to diagnose and treat any such problem from developing.

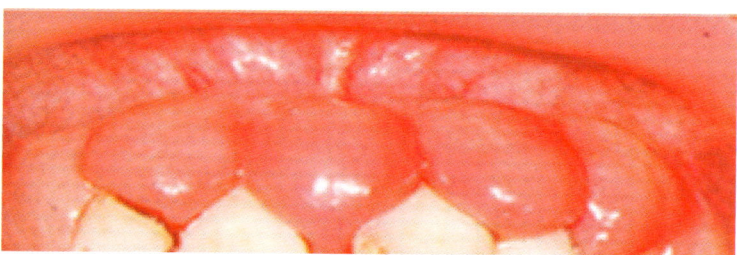

Fig. 1.2 Swelling in Gums During Pregnancy

3. **Dietary habits:** Pregnancy brings along with it behavioural changes and cravings. The mother can experience increased urge for sweet or sour foods. Due to change in dietary habits and frequent snacking on foods like sweets, biscuits, colas, and chips that are high in sugar content, there is an increase in the chances of cavity formation as these foods are conducive for the growth and attachment of bacteria to the teeth. Controlled eating habits and proper oral hygiene routine are of great importance. Hence, I emphasize upon the importance of a regular dental check-up during pregnancy.

4. **Damage due to morning sickness:** Most women, during pregnancy, experience morning sickness. The increased frequency of vomiting causes increase in the acidic content of the mouth. This causes the leaching of calcium from the enamel of the teeth, making them vulnerable to pitting and cavity formation. If brushing is causing increased nausea, change the toothpaste to a bland tasting one. Rinse your mouth thoroughly after vomiting, either with water or a mouth wash. Do not use toothpaste just after vomiting as it can damage the tooth surface. These simple actions can go a long way in the prevention of dental problems.

5. **Dental treatment during pregnancy:** Minor dental procedures, like scaling or cleaning of teeth, should be done in the second trimester of pregnancy (fourth to sixth month). The dentist **must** be informed regarding the pregnancy and the medication that the patient is taking, so that only

drugs safe for use during pregnancy are prescribed, and that too, if they cannot be avoided. Dental X-rays should be avoided or else lead shield with safety collar should be used to protect the baby from radiation. Machines with low radiation should be used wherever possible. Digital X-rays (RVG) available today produce much lower radiation. Exposure to such ionizing radiation can cause genetic defects in the baby, hence caution and judicious use of X-rays is advised.

Maternal Dental Care and Effect on the Developing Baby's Teeth and Birth

The foundation for strong teeth is laid in the womb. The first evidence of formation of the milk teeth is in the sixth week of intrauterine life (that is, in the womb). The bud formation of the permanent tooth starts in the fourth or fifth month of intrauterine life. This clearly explains the role of a good, well-balanced diet, rich in minerals, vitamins, and trace elements.

Research shows that gum disease in the mother's mouth can result in babies with low birth weight and early (premature) delivery due to prostaglandins, a chemical released by oral bacteria.

The need and importance of regular and comprehensive dental care during pregnancy is obvious. The bacteria responsible for cavity formation in teeth are passed on to the baby from the mother and even low grade infection in the mother can cause low weight babies and also premature deliveries.

From Bud to Tooth
Eruption and Shedding of Teeth

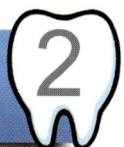

*D*evelopment of the milk teeth starts in the sixth week of intra uterine life (in the mother's womb). But they are visible in the mouth only as early as six months after birth of the baby. In rare cases, children are born with a tooth or two. These are called "neonatal teeth". They are not true teeth but thickened or calcified gum tissue. In the interest of the child, such a tooth should be removed, just in case it detaches while suckling and gets stuck in the wind pipe of the infant. It can also pose a problem in the feeding of the child as it bites into the breast tissue of the mother and may cause injury.

The process of emergence or breaking through of the teeth through the gums in the mouth is called **eruption**. Teeth erupt twice in a lifetime and can be divided into two types:

1. **Primary or Milk Teeth:**
   These are the first teeth to erupt in the mouth. They are twenty in number and eruption starts any time after six months of age. There are **incisors** or biting teeth, **canines** or tearing teeth and **molars** or chewing teeth. The premolars are not present in the primary set of teeth. (Figure/Chart)

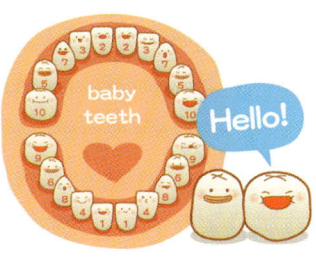

Fig. 2.1 Milk Teeth

2. **Secondary or Permanent or Succedaneous Teeth:** They are the successor of the primary teeth and are thirty two in number. Their eruption should be preceded with the shedding or falling out or exfoliation of the primary or milk teeth. The exception being the molars, which erupt behind the milk teeth as the size of the jaw increases with age. This set has incisors, canines, premolar**s** and molars.

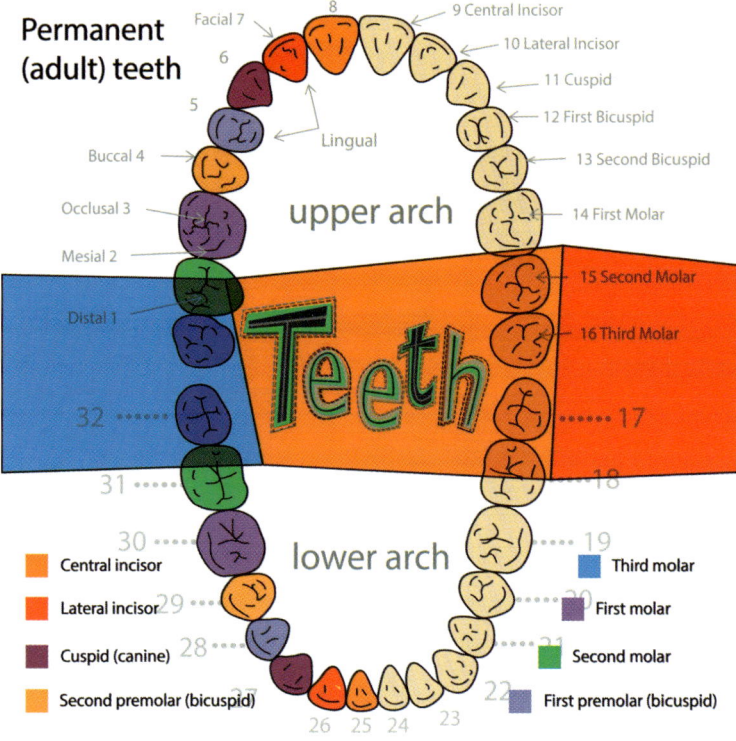

Fig. 2.2 Permanent Teeth

The chart below lists the eruption and shedding sequence of primary and permanent teeth:

Primary or Milk Teeth

Tooth type	Eruption time	Shedding time
Upper teeth		
Central incisor	08–10 months	06–07 years
Lateral incisor	09–13 months	07–08 years
Canine	16–22 months	10–12 years
First molar	13–19 months	09–11 years
Second molar	25–33 months	10–12 years
Lower teeth		
Central incisor	06–10 months	06–07 years
Lateral incisor	10–16 months	07–08 years
Canine	17–23 months	09–12 years
First molar	14–18 months	09–11 years
Second molar	23–31 months	10–12 years

Secondary or Permanent Teeth

Tooth type	Eruption	Root completion
Upper teeth		
Central incisor	07–08 years	10–11 years
Lateral incisor	08–09 years	11–12 years
Canine	11–12 years	14–15 years
First premolar	10–11 years	13–14 years
Second premolar	11–12 years	13–15 years
First molar	05–06 years	08–10 years
Second molar	12–13 years	15–16 years
Third molar or wisdom tooth	17–21 years	19–23 years

Lower teeth		
Central incisor	06–07 years	90–10 years
Lateral incisor	07–08 years	10–11 years
Canine	09–10 years	12–13 years
First premolar	10–12 years	13–15 years
Second premolar	11–12 years	14–15 years
First molar	05–07 years	08–10 years
Second molar	11–13 years	14–16 years
Third molar or wisdom tooth	17–21 years	19–23 years

These dates are listed here just to give you an idea about the eruption and shedding of teeth. In cases where a delay is seen in either the eruption or shedding of teeth, it is in the best interest of the child to see a dentist and take an expert opinion.

A few problems seen at this stage, which warrant immediate attention, are listed below:

1. **Neonatal teeth:** As explained earlier, these teeth, in rare cases, are present at the time of the birth. Or they may erupt in the first month of the baby's life. They are usually removed to prevent accidental swallowing and difficulty in feeding.

2. **Delayed shedding of milk teeth:** This occurs when the permanent tooth erupts before the milk tooth has fallen as it may be positioned behind the milk tooth. If a condition like this is noticed by the

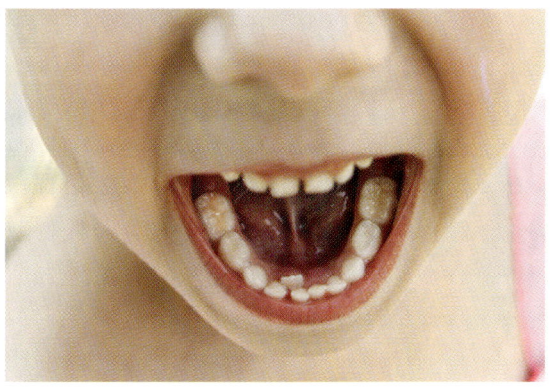

Fig. 2.3 Milk Tooth Not Fallen, Permanent Tooth Coming Out

parents, they need to consult a dentist and have the milk tooth removed to prevent the permanent tooth from becoming crooked. The normal sequence of events involves shedding of the milk tooth due to its root getting dissolved, followed by the eruption of the permanent tooth. A change in this sequence can lead to the permanent teeth being crooked and abnormally placed, due to lack of space for it to erupt.

3. **Premature loss of primary teeth:** Sometimes the milk teeth are prematurely lost due to decay or trauma. Such a condition is responsible for the closure of space which is meant for

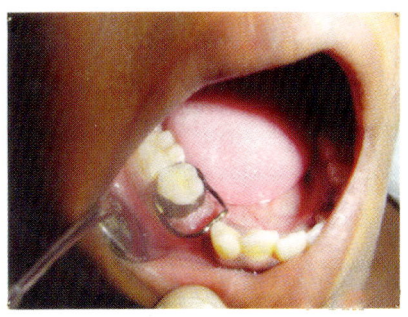

Fig. 2.4 Space Maintainer Appliance

the permanent tooth. In a condition like this, a Space Maintainer appliance should be used to prevent space closure and crowding of teeth at a later stage. (Figures) This is yet another condition where you need to see your dentist without delay.

4. **Permanent teeth not erupting:** At times you will find that it has been a long time, say more than a month, since the child lost the milk tooth but the permanent tooth is just not coming out. In these cases, an intra-oral radiograph (X-ray) is taken by the dentist to confirm whether the successor permanent tooth is present in the bone. At times, a fibrous band or thickened gum tissue present over the tooth prevents the tooth from erupting. Once this is confirmed, the dentist might decide to give a small incision or cut in the gums in that region to allow the underlying tooth to come out. This is a painless, minor procedure and usually done under local anaesthesia.

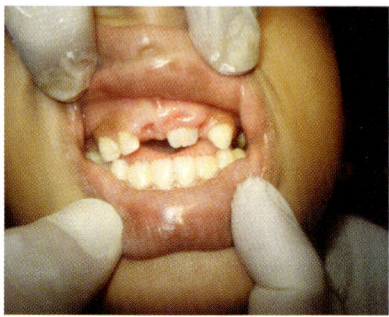

Fig. 2.5 Non Erupting Permanent Teeth

Hello! I Am Your Tooth
The Chewing Apparatus

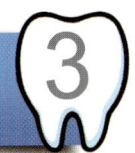

𝒟o you know that the jaws, the gums, and the teeth are the three major parts of the chewing apparatus or what helps us in eating food?

The Jaws: The upper and the lower are the two jaws which house the teeth. The upper jaw is called the **Maxilla** and the lower jaw is called the **Mandible**. They provide the foundation in which the tooth bud develops and grows. The jaw bone can be divided into two parts, one part that forms the body and second part that anchors the teeth and holds them in place. (Figures)

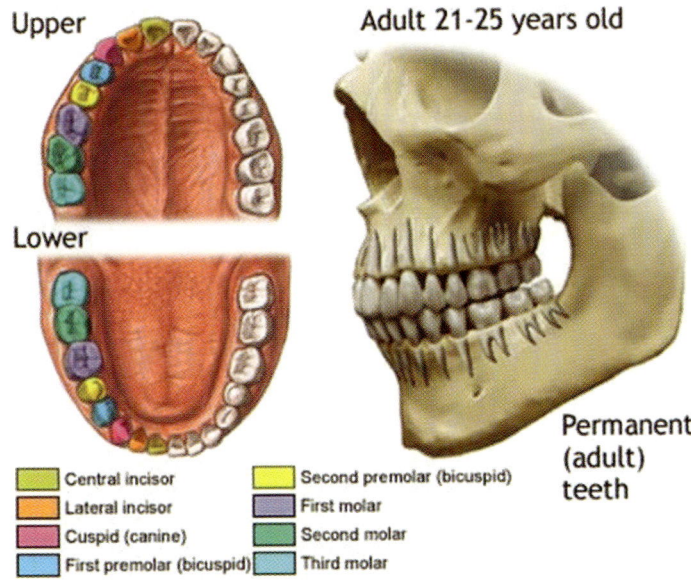

Fig. 3.1

The Gums: Technically called the **Gingiva**, it is the soft outer layer covering the bone. It is visible to the eye as a coral pink layer. The gum also forms a collar around the teeth and is attached to the teeth at their neck. There is a shallow pocket (Sulcus), formed at the junction of the tooth and gums, which is a blind area and harbours food and plaque, hence bacteria. For total oral hygiene, it needs to be cleaned thoroughly during brushing. (Figures)

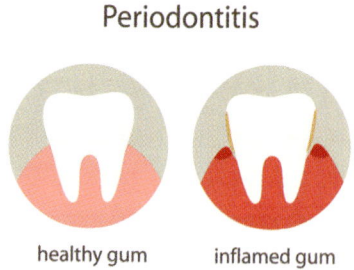

Fig. 3.2 Gums

The Teeth: The term tooth we all are aware of, but what we may not know is that this tooth is embedded in the bone. It is the bone that gives it strength. The tooth has two parts, namely, the **Crown**, which is seen in the mouth, and the **Root** which is embedded in the jaw bone. The outer part of the crown is covered with a whitish layer of enamel. **Enamel** is the hardest tissue in the human body and prevents the tooth from the attack of cavity-forming bacteria. The enamel has no sensation. It protects the inner sensitive parts from hot and cold foods or fluids, and provides the necessary chewing strength to the tooth. The outer layer of the root is called **Cementum,** which is relatively softer and helps

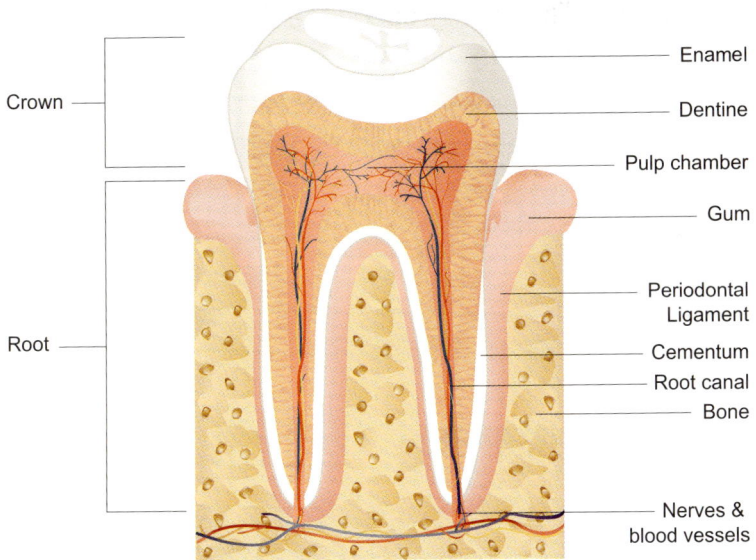

Fig. 3.3 Different Parts of a Tooth

in bonding with the bone. The **Dentine** lies beneath the enamel and cementum layers. In a healthy tooth, this layer is fully protected from the outside environment as it has nerves close to it. However, once exposed, it is responsible for the sensations felt by us while eating or drinking cold, sweet, or sour foodstuff. It is a softer layer and easily attacked by cavity-forming bacteria. The core of the tooth is hollow, containing the vital **Pulp tissue**, which is a mesh of nerves and blood vessels entering through a tiny hole at the tip of the root. Once this pulp region is exposed, we start feeling pain with hot fluids, like tea or coffee. (Figures)

Tongue: Another important organ in the mouth is the tongue. It does not form the chewing apparatus but plays an integral role in the chewing cycle within the mouth. It is made up of muscles and has a rich supply of nerves and blood vessels. It helps in the manipulation of food during chewing and swallowing. It is the primary organ for taste as it is covered by taste buds. It is also responsible for speech and, with the teeth, leads to the production of different sounds. It also forms a natural

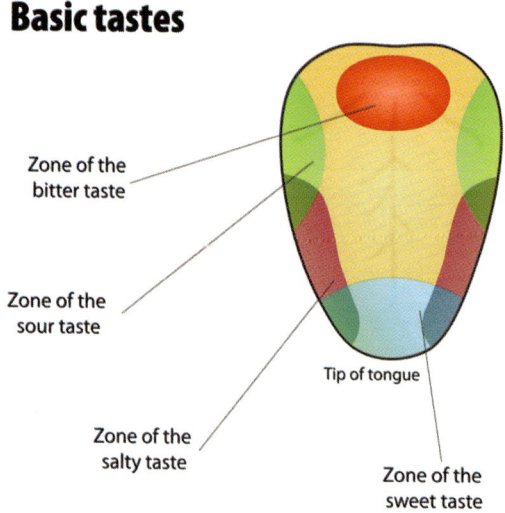

Fig. 3.4

mechanism for the cleansing of teeth. Some children start speaking very late or may stutter or stammer, the reason for this may be "Tongue tie" (Figure). In this condition, the tongue is attached firmly to the floor of the mouth by a band of tissue. This needs to be snipped to free the tongue movement and allow a normal speaking pattern.

Milk Teeth and Their Importance

Is it not true that the very day a child puts something in his or her mouth or is drooling, we think it's because the teeth are about to erupt? The commonly used term for this is teething, that is, the eruption of the milk teeth. The teeth do not cut the gums and come out, rather they gently slide their way into the mouth without any trauma to the gums. The eruption of milk teeth (also called primary teeth) usually begins at the age of about six months, though there may be some variation. In most cases, teething may cause no distress to the child or to the parents, but sometimes there may be local (in the mouth) or systemic (generally seen in the body) effects. These effects are:

Local signs

1. Swelling of gums
2. Drooling of saliva
3. Flushing of skin

Drooling of saliva is the most common symptom seen in almost all children who are in the process of teething. This drooling of saliva can cause a rash on the baby's sensitive skin of the face. This needs

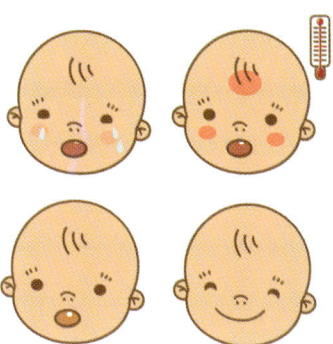

Fig. 4.1 Symptoms of Teething

to be cleaned with warm water, patted dry, and a mild lubricant lotion or oil should be applied. The drooling can be excessive at times and can travel to the back of the throat and cause gagging and irritating cough.

Systemic signs

1. Loss of appetite or not feeling hungry
2. Crying without any known reason
3. Sleeplessness
4. Diarrhoea
5. Fever

The teething baby may sometimes suffer from fever and diarrhoea. It the fever is above 101° F, an appropriate dose of paracetamol should be given *only after consulting a Child Specialist or a Dentist.* The itching gums need something soothing and a cool spoon, popsicle, or teething rings can work well to give relief.

The lower front teeth are the first ones to erupt, followed by the upper front teeth and then, one by one, the rest of the teeth come out. We have a total of about 20 teeth as babies and it takes about 2 to 3 years for all of them to come out (as given in chapter 2).

Importance of Milk Teeth

Most parents feel that the milk teeth are not important as they will eventually fall off. Hence, even on noticing brown or black discolouration on the teeth, it is neglected. A word of caution for these parents—you are overlooking a small problem and will be hit by the bigger one later! This will be in the form of swelling and pain.

And that, dear friends, is bad news for all—the child, the parents, and the dentist. Management of decayed and disintegrated teeth, especially in small children, is not an easy task even for the most experienced dentist. *We must avoid reaching such a situation!* Believe me, we can, if we are careful and alert in the beginning.

Reasons to Save Milk Teeth

1. Milk teeth help your child to chew food and gain nutrition, which helps in growth and prevents nutritional deficiencies in the body.
2. They are the forerunners of permanent teeth as they make way for them.
3. They maintain space for the permanent teeth. If lost early, there can be crowding of permanent teeth which appear crooked, requiring orthodontic treatment (braces) in the future.
4. They provide stimulus to the upper and lower jaws and help them grow normally.
5. Mutilated teeth are aesthetically not pleasing and can have psychological effects for the child.

The Monster Dental Caries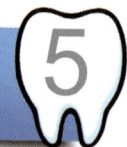

*D*ental caries is one of the most prevalent problems in children these days. It is more commonly seen in the affluent classes. The reason is the much higher consumption of processed foods and sugar-laden products. The accumulation of refined sugars on the tooth surface provides a good medium for the growth of caries-producing bacteria. These bacteria produce acids which attack and demineralize the tooth enamel causing pitting, which is the starting point of dental caries or tooth decay.

Stages of Dental Caries or Tooth Decay (Diagram/Figures)

1. **Stage 1:** This is the initial stage of dental caries, where the demineralization of the enamel takes place and there is formation of a pit.

   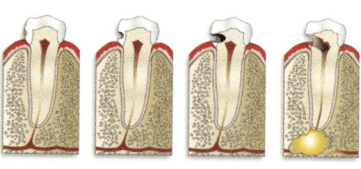
   Fig. 5.1 Progression of Cavity

2. **Stage 2:** In this stage, the cavity progresses into the dentine, or the layer beneath the enamel.

3. **Stage 3:** Now the cavity travels further, but it still does not affected the pulp or the nerve tissue; but the tooth becomes sensitive.

4. **Stage 4:** The caries now advance to the nerve and the irreversible process of destruction of nerve tissue starts.
5. **Stage 5:** The nerve becomes totally dead and this causes infection in the bone and soft tissue around the root of the tooth. There can be formation of a pus-filled abscess as well.

Reasons of Tooth Decay

- **Nursing bottle caries**

Children who drink milk with a bottle and usually fall asleep with the bottle in the mouth, or move around with sugary pacifiers in their mouth, are at a risk of dental caries. This particular type of caries affects the upper front teeth initially and then spreads to the upper back teeth. The lower teeth remain unaffected as they are covered by the tongue.

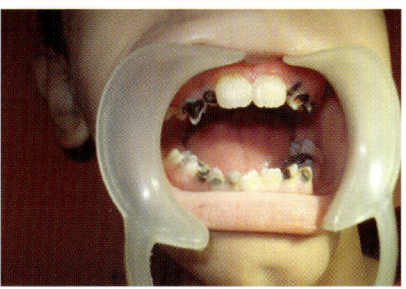

Fig. 5.2

This type of decay spreads rapidly as the tooth material of the milk teeth is relatively soft. Unrestricted and excessive breast feeding can also lead to nursing bottle caries. The weaning from bottle and breast feeding should start with the completion of the first year. Feeding of the child should be done before he or she falls asleep.

- **Sugary diet**

High consumption of sugary and sticky foods, foods rich in starch, and increased use of foods like candies, biscuits, colas and canned juices are reasons for the starting of tooth decay. The soft structural material of the milk teeth offers little resistance to the rapid spread of the cavity, both deep into the tooth as well as into the adjoining teeth. Management of deeply carious milk teeth successfully is one of the greatest challenges faced by the dentist.

Fig. 5.3 Foods Containing Sugars

Symptoms of Dental Caries

Children usually cannot catch the early symptoms of dental cavities, which are sensitivity to cold or sweet fluids and foods. They usually start complaining only when there is pain while eating or drinking these food items. But the sad part is that the pain only appears when the decay has progressed close to the nerve, or there is swelling of the gums and pus formation. In extreme cases, the child may develop fever as the infection may spread through the body.

Diagnosing Dental Caries

Early diagnosis of cavities can make treatment really easy for both the child and the parent. But timely diagnosis is only possible if the child visits the dentist at least every six months, otherwise the early symptoms of cavity formation go unnoticed. Listed here are a few tips for the diagnosis of dental caries:

- Keep inspecting your child's teeth, under good light, on a regular basis. Use a small spoon or an ice-cream stick to move the cheeks or tongue for easy visibility.

- Appearance of brown or black spots on the tooth surface should ring an alarm bell, indicating cavity formation.

- Look out for the child's complaints of discomfort or pain on chewing or intake of sweets or hot and cold foods.

If any of the above symptoms are noticed, a dentist should be consulted immediately. The dentist, with the help of mouth mirrors and probe, will be able to diagnose cavities or any other problem, if present. The depth of the cavity can be assessed with the help of a radiograph (intraoral X-ray/RVG), where required.

Treatment of Dental Caries

Treatment modalities for cavities differs depending on the stage or progress of dental caries.

Stages 1 and 2: Treatment is relatively simple at these stages. The dentist cleans the tooth of the decayed material and then the cavity is shaped for receiving a filling or a restoration. Different materials can be used for filling the cavity. The dentist can use materials like silver amalgam, glass ionomer cement, or composite resin, depending on the requirement.

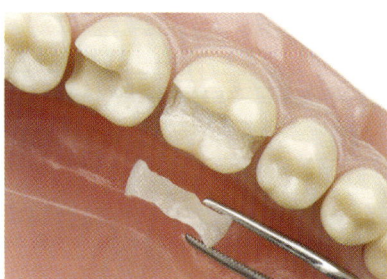
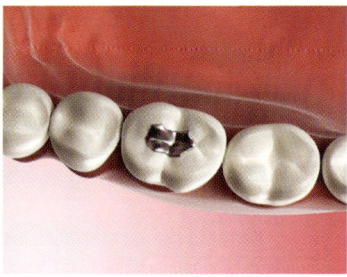

Fig. 5.4 Tooth Coloured Filling Material

Fig. 5.5 Silver Amalgam Filling Material

Stage 3: Once the cavity reaches this stage, the caries is removed without exposing the nerve tissue and a fluoride-releasing filling, such as glass ionomer cement, that remineralizes the tooth structure, can be done. This is called **Atraumatic Restorative Technique**.

Stage 4: In deciduous teeth, the exposure of the pulp necessitates treatment of the pulp or nerve tissue. Once affected, the nerve begins to die and this degenerative process cannot be stopped. The child needs medication to combat pain and infection to provide relief first, followed by **Root Canal Treatment (RCT)** to maintain the tooth trouble-free in the mouth. Once the RCT is completed, the tooth is restored with a permanent filling. A crown may be placed on the tooth to allow it to serve its full time till the permanent tooth erupts.

In permanent teeth, where the dental caries has progressed so deep but the root formation of these permanent teeth is not complete, pulp may not be removed. This procedure is called **Pulpotomy**. Where the complete pulp tissue is removed, it is called Pulpectomy. The intention is to let the root grow to its complete size and shape. Once the root formation is complete, as assessed from an X-ray, a proper RCT is done and the tooth is restored with the placement of a crown.

Stage 5: The first line of treatment is to provide relief from pain with the help of analgesics and antibiotics. It has been observed that once there is abscess formation due to death of the pulpal tissue, the chances of success of root canal treatment are greatly reduced in deciduous teeth or milk teeth. In such a condition, the tooth may have to be removed. A space maintainer device is used, which prevents the closure of space meant for the permanent teeth. In the permanent tooth, RCT has to be performed to save the tooth, followed by a crown.

Explanation of Terms

When the tooth decay has advanced to the nerve tissue or pulp, as we call it, especially in young permanent teeth with immature roots and also in milk teeth which need to be retained as space maintainers for their successors that is, the permanent teeth, the integrity of the nerve tissue, as well as the tooth structure which is lost, needs to be restored. The treatment of the pulp tissue can be varied, depending on whether the pulp is vital or nonvital. This will be done by the dentist and the best line of treatment will be advised. This can be indirect pulp capping, direct pulp capping, Pulpotomy, and Pulpectomy.

Indirect Pulp Capping

When there is extensive caries but no symptoms like pain or sensitivity, caries surrounding the pulp is left in place to avoid pulp exposure and is covered with a biocompatible material. Over that, a filling is done.

Direct pulp capping

When a pinpoint exposure of the pulp is encountered during cavity preparation or following a traumatic injury, a biocompatible base may be placed in contact with the exposed pulp tissue. The tooth is then restored with a material that seals the tooth completely. Sometimes there may be pain or sensitivity after the procedure. In such a case, additional treatment may be advised by the dentist.

Pulpotomy

A pulpotomy is performed in a milk tooth with extensive caries involving the pulp of the crown of the tooth, without involvement of the pulp of the root. The coronal pulp is amputated, and the remaining vital root pulp tissue surface is treated with long-term clinically-successful medicaments. The object is to hold the tooth in the mouth till the time the permanent tooth is in a position to erupt.

Pulpectomy (conventional root canal treatment) RCT

Pulpectomy in milk teeth or permanent teeth, where the root formation is complete, is the conventional root canal treatment, which may be done for exposed, infected

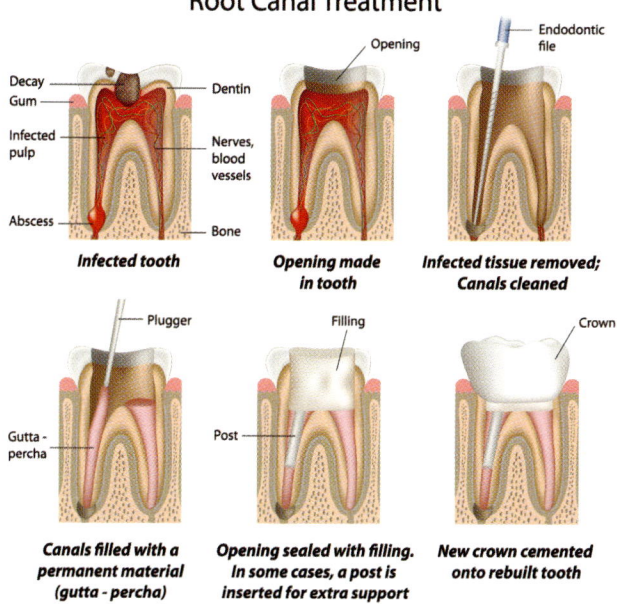

Fig. 5.6

teeth to eliminate infection. During the procedure, a hole is made in the tooth to gain access to the pulp chamber and the root canals. The entire infected pulp tissue is removed. The canals are then cleaned, shaped, and disinfected. An inert material is used to fill the canals and prevent further infections. This is followed by a filling of the tooth and a fixing a cap to protect the tooth from damage due to the force of chewing.

Steps for the Prevention of Dental Caries

These steps are applicable both for milk teeth as well as permanent teeth.

- A good oral hygiene routine is essential for the prevention of dental caries.
- Taking a diet rich in fibrous foods and avoiding sugars and sticky food, especially before going to bed.
- Fluoride in oral hygiene products (toothpaste or mouthwash) and fluoride treatment in the dentist's clinic.
- In teeth with deep pits and grooves, application of pit and fissure sealants may work wonders.
- Regular visit to the dentist— at least once every six months

Pit and Fissure Sealants

The pit and fissure sealants play an integral part in the prevention of dental caries. Teeth which have deep pits and fissures catch food debris easily. Hence there are greater chances of growth of bacteria and subsequent formation of cavities. Using minimal preparation of the tooth, a composite resin is used to fill these pits and fissures, so that food debris is not retained in them and no cavity formation takes place. (Diagrams)

Reasons for Tooth Decay

I commonly encounter this question from both patients and friends. The answers are simple.

- Bottle feeding or pacifiers.
- Increased frequency of consumption of sweets, cola, fizzy drinks, biscuits, chips, and so on.
- Poor oral hygiene due to lack of proper brushing of teeth, which leads to accumulation of plaque and food particles on the teeth.
- Administration of sweetened medicated syrups (sugar-free syrups are available now).
- Genetic factors.

Prevention of Dental Caries or Cavities

1. **Visit to the dentist:** I advocate strongly the importance of a regular, six-monthly visit to the dentist. This will lead to an early diagnosis of budding caries and other problems, which can be dealt with early and the action can be taken before it gets too late. These visits also help in building trust between the child and the dentist and to ward off any fear regarding the dentist in the child's mind. *Fear of the dentist is one of the major hurdles in the management of a child patient.*

2. **Bottle feeding or pacifiers:** Bottle feeding and the use of pacifiers should be discouraged. The milk that is left in the mouth after feeding the

child with the bottle undergoes fermentation and causes bacterial growth, which leads to cavities. But wherever it is unavoidable, a few precautions should be taken:

a) After feeding, always give the child a few drops of water to wash away the residue or left-over milk in the mouth.

b) The baby should be in a reclining position at the time of feeding to assist in the drainage of milk and prevent its pooling in the mouth.

c) Weaning from the milk bottle and introduction of cup or sipper should be done at the earliest.

3. **Diet:** Increased frequency of consumption of sweets, colas, biscuits, chips, and so on, is harmful to the health of the teeth. These items contain high amounts of refined sugars, which undergo fermentation and consequentially result in cavities. Increased intake of fibrous diet such as fruits and green vegetables act as a "detergent" diet and their consumption should be encouraged. Colas and fizzy drinks contain acid that erodes the protective enamel layer on the teeth, making attack by the cavity-forming bacteria easier. If consumed, use of a straw is advised as it allows minimum exposure of teeth to the drink.

4. **Brushing and oral hygiene:** Poor oral hygiene due to lack of proper brushing of teeth is a very important cause for dental caries. If not cleaned properly, the food particles remain attached to the tooth surface and lead to the increase of bacterial

count in the mouth, resulting in pitting of teeth and cavity formation. It is of utmost importance to inculcate in our children the habit of brushing twice a day, once in the morning and once before going to bed. *Night-time brushing is more important as the food material stays in the mouth for the whole night, providing a good breeding ground for the harmful bacteria.*

The amount of paste being used and the way it is applied onto the brush is also important. Use paste about the size of a pea, and press the tube over the brush to flow the paste between the bristles. (as shown in the diagrams) Paste placed on top of the bristles gets washed away as soon as we start brushing. Children, at times, tend to swallow the paste while brushing, so excess paste is not advisable. Teach your child to keep spitting out the froth during brushing and not to swallow it.

5. **Fluoride:** Fluoride plays an important role in the prevention of dental caries. The fluoride binds with the enamel of the teeth to make it resistant to the attack of bacteria. We should make sure that there is fluoride present in our tooth paste. Six-monthly application of fluoride at the dental care centre or clinic can be of immense value in the prevention of cavities in children.

One cautionary note with toothpastes is that regular pastes contain more fluoride (1000 ppm) which is not required for children. Today, toothpastes are specially formulated for children as they contain the right amount of fluoride (500 ppm).

Eating for a Juicy Smile
Nutrition, Diet, and Dentistry

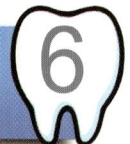

The role of nutrition and diet has been emphasized in a previous chapter of this book. But it is not wrong to say that whatever has been said about this topic can be augmented.

Vitamins and minerals have been proven for their therapeutic value. The role of a nutritious diet starts right from the time of conception. The mother needs at least 1,000 mg of elementary calcium every day. A diet rich in calcium, vitamins, and minerals helps in the formation of healthy teeth and gums as well. However, a diet rich in sugar and acid is harmful for the teeth.

Role of Calcium

The role of calcium in the development of teeth, bones, and for contraction of muscles has been proved. It is also a proven fact that children who consume lesser than the required dose of calcium are more prone to periodontitis, a bacterial disease which damages the tissue and bone supporting the tooth.

The calcium taken after tooth formation has completed (during the teenages) is neither imbibed nor taken up by the tooth. Hence, the role of calcium for the development of teeth is only during childhood, probably up to the teenage years. Starting around age nine, the children need almost twice as much calcium as younger kids.

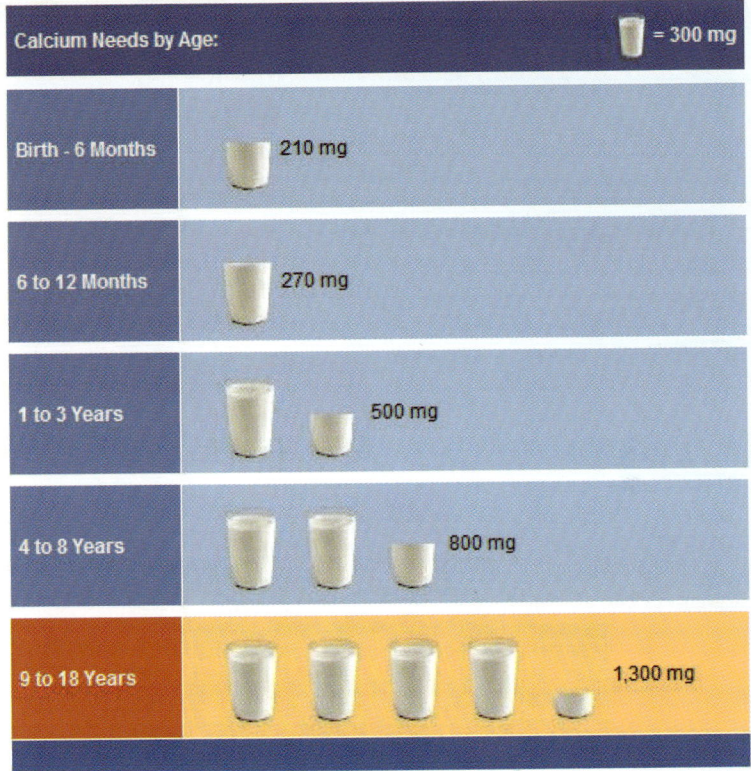

Source: DRI for Calcium, NAS 1997

Fig. 6.1

The best source of calcium is milk and milk products, while other non-dairy natural sources are dark green leafy vegetables such as broccoli, spinach, and bok choy.

Other foods like calcium fortified tofu, soy beverages, cereals, and orange juice have calcium added to them. For children showing lactose intolerance, these non-dairy dietary sources are of great significance. Calcium supplements can also be incorporated in the diet.

Vitamin D

The role of vitamin D has been demonstrated in the absorption of calcium by the body tissues and we already know the importance of calcium. Vitamin D is also called "sunshine vitamin" as it is absorbed from the sunlight through the skin. It is stored in the fat cells of the body and used when required. A daily exposure to sunlight for 10–15 minutes, without sunscreen and arms exposed, is enough to gain the required dose of vitamin D. Another good source of this vitamin is fortified milk yoghurt.

Vitamin C

Vitamin C plays an important role in the development of the immune system and wound repair. It is also known for its importance in the maintenance of bone tissue and teeth. Diet deficient in vitamin C can lead to a disease called scurvy. Although not seen much today, this disease is characterized by bleeding and painful gums. This may be seen in children who are on mother's milk exclusively for an abnormally long time. All citrus fruits like lemon, oranges, and grapes are rich sources of vitamin C. Oral supplements, like tablets, are also available and may be taken when prescribed by a dentist or a physician.

Other Vitamins and Micro Nutrients

Fats, though demonized, are also essential for proper growth and development of children. An important factor that most people are unaware of is that you must have adequate essential fats present in your diet in order to get the calcium from your bloodstream into your bones.

Carbohydrates

Carbohydrates (carbs), when consumed frequently and excessively, are harmful for the teeth. Carbs disintegrate into sugar which, when in contact with the tooth surface for a long time, causes cavities. Sugars are a good breeding ground for the cavity-forming bacteria to produce acid and decay the enamel surface.

This does not mean you have to give up carbs totally! Just try to eat them only at or before meals. Carbs are sticky substances, so they tend to stick between teeth or below the gum line. Eating your carbs at mealtime will give you a chance to clean the carbs from the teeth. The more you eat, the more saliva you produce and saliva helps wash food particles away. Fruits are known as detergent diets as they help in cleaning the surface of the teeth.

Dietary Habits for Oral Health

1. Limit the use of candies, biscuits, and sticky foods. If you cannot avoid them, then brush after eating them.
2. Avoid the use of carbonated or aerated drinks, rich in sugars. When drinking aerated drinks do so at one go instead of sipping. Use a straw.
3. Avoid binging on carbohydrate-rich diet between meals. Limit eating such foodstuff at meal time.
4. For mid-day snacks, eat fruits and salads.
5. Drinking water frequently during the day causes the mouth to be free of bacterial deposits.

We Call Them Bad—Habits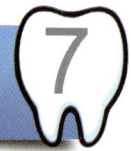

*E*veryone has seen a baby sucking their thumb, or a child biting their nails. Well, let me tell you that all these things that look very sweet on the baby at that age are potential problems in the long run. Their early identification and treatment can save you from a lot of trouble later on. Listed below are habits which are detrimental in the long run.

1. Thumb or Finger Sucking

Thumb sucking is a normal habit but can become a problem if it continues for a long time. Thumb sucking has different relevance for different children. It can just be a way of satisfying their hunger. For some it is nothing more than a habit, for some it is an emotional crutch to cope with feelings of insecurity.

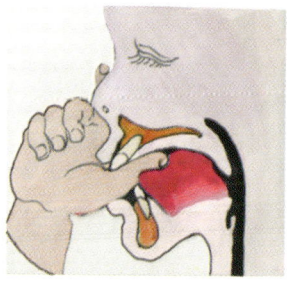

Fig. 7.1 Pressure on the upper teeth due Thumb sucking.

Normally this habit should stop between 4–6 years of age. Persistence of the habit even after the eruption of permanent teeth can have deleterious effects on the teeth and other structures in the mouth.

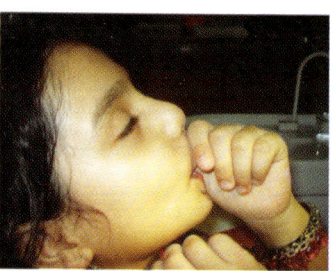

Fig. 7.2

Effects of thumb sucking

1. Front teeth become protruded
2. Crowding, crooked teeth or open bite (upper and lower front teeth not in contact)
3. Speech problem
4. In severe cases, the whole of the front part of the upper jaw can get pulled forward resulting in a bone defect

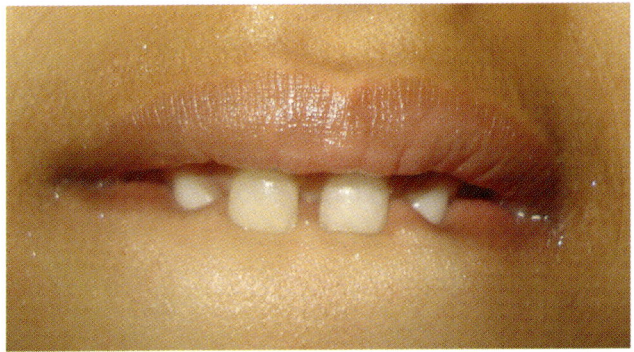

Fig. 7.3 Front Teeth Coming Out

Tips to prevent and stop the habit

1. Make the baby wear mittens.
2. Keep the baby's hands occupied with toys, etc.
3. Check the baby whenever you notice him or her sucking the thumb
4. Remove thumb from the mouth when the baby is sleeping
5. Keep the baby happy and comfortable so that a feeling of insecurity does not set in.

6. Put to rest the child's fears by talking to the child and explaining the doubts to him or her.
7. Educate the child that the thumb carries a lot of germs which get into the body because of thumb sucking and can cause diseases.
8. Reward the child for listening to you and not sucking the thumb.
9. If all this does not work, consult the dentist regarding an appliance to break the habit, which can be fixed or removable.

2. Tongue Thrusting

In the first four months of the baby's life, tongue thrusting is a safety mechanism. It works by pushing outwards whatever is placed in the mouth and prevents the baby from choking. It also helps the baby to suck milk by pressing the nipple between the tongue and upper gum pads.

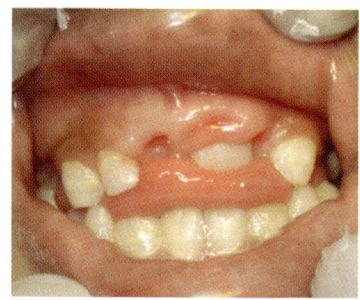

Fig. 7.4 Notice the tongue being thrust between the teeth

But once the child has grown up and suckling is not required, the tongue thrusting or infantile suckling pattern should automatically change to the adult swallowing mechanism where the tongue comes in contact with the palate and not the teeth. If this does not happen and the infantile suckling pattern continues, it is called Tongue Thrusting.

Effects of Tongue Thrusting

1. Proclination or protrusion of teeth.
2. Anterior teeth/front teeth do not contact one another.
3. Lips do not meet, which can lead to gum problems.
4. Development of gaps between the teeth and later loosening of teeth.

Tips to correct Tongue Thrusting

1. Do not lick lips before swallowing.
2. Do not place tongue between the teeth at the time of swallowing. Instead, place the tongue in contact with the roof of the mouth or palate during swallowing.
3. If all this does not work, seek professional help. The dentist will make a removable habit breaking appliance which has to be worn to correct the pattern of swallowing and train the tongue into the new position.

3. Bruxism

The grinding or clenching of teeth is called Bruxism. This is commonly seen in adults but also seen in a few children. This habit is destructive for both primary and permanent teeth. If noticed, it should be addressed at the earliest.

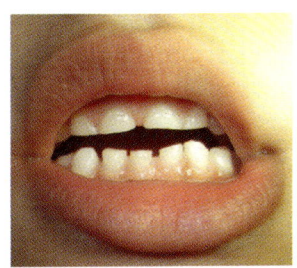

Fig. 7.5 Teeth have got worn off due to Bruxism

Symptoms

1. Wearing off of teeth, especially front teeth
2. Teeth become loose
3. Sounds of grinding in the night
4. Chipping away of teeth edges
5. Teeth become sensitive to cold foods and fluids

Treatment

In children, bruxism can be treated by reassurance and a constant vigil. Keep a constant check on the child and make them aware of the clenching.

It gets corrected as the child grows old.

In some cases, this might persist in adulthood and can cause excessive wearing of teeth, periodontal damage, and muscle fatigue.

In cases where the habit is causing harmful effects on the teeth, jaws and muscles of face, a soft device called Nightguard can be made by the dentist for the child to wear over his or her teeth at night, or even during the daytime if the habit is severe.

Fig. 7.6 Front Teeth Coming Out

4. Mouth Breathing

The process of inhaling and exhaling of air is called breathing. When this process is performed by the mouth instead of the nose, it is called Mouth Breathing.

Reasons for mouth breathing

1. Obstruction in the nose, hampering smooth and effortless breathing, for example, adenoids, nasal polyps, deviated nasal septum, and narrow nasal apertures.
2. Chronic allergy and infections.
3. Lower jaw pushed back due to thumb sucking and excessive use of pacifiers.

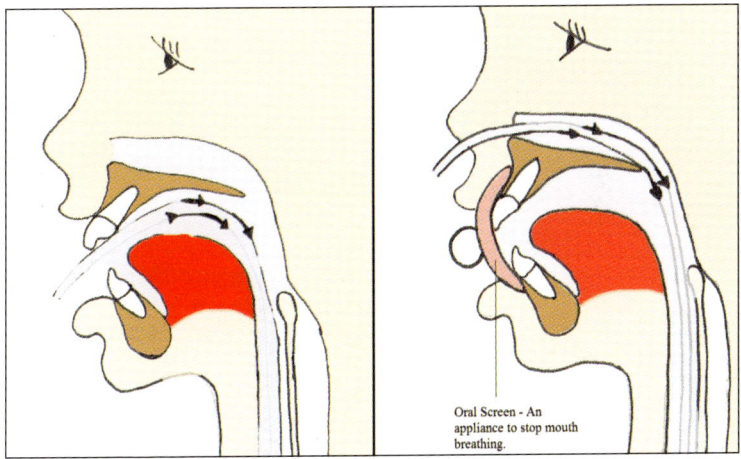

Fig. 7.7 (a) Mouth Breather
      (b) Oral screen being used to correct mouth breathing

Diagnosing mouth breathing

1. Cover the mouth with your hand for 30 sec. If the child is a mouth breather or partially mouth and partially nose breather, he or she will find it difficult to breathe or will compensate by taking deep breaths.
2. In infants, observe the baby's feeding pattern. In mouth breathers, the baby will have to stop feeding from time to time from the bottle or breast to draw in air.

Consequences of mouth breathing

1. Low immunity in children with this habit
2. Deformity of the face and jaws, for example, long face, high palate
3. Crooked teeth
4. Bad breath and dryness of gums
5. Disruption in sleep pattern and lack of concentration

Treatment

1. Address the problem of obstruction in the nose by consulting an ENT specialist.
2. Deep breathing exercises.
3. Using a habit breaking appliance, like oral screen, fabricated by the dentist.
4. In cases where the habit is because of the backward position of the lower jaw, a corrective (myofuctional) appliance is advised by the dentist.

5. Nail Biting

Nail biting is usually a result of nervousness and insecurity. Most parents feel it is harmless in kids, hence it goes unattended. But let me inform you, this is a habit which needs to be nipped in the bud. If not done at an early age, it will carry on into adulthood.

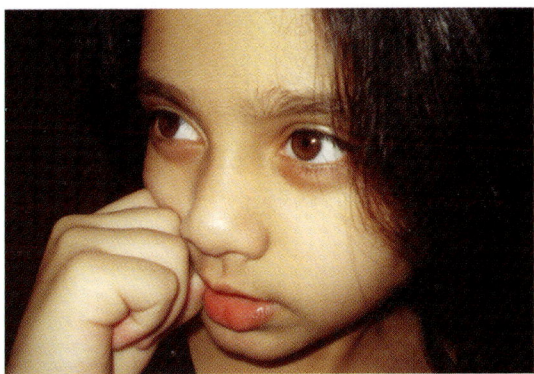

Fig. 7.8 Child biting nails

Harmful effects of nail biting

1. It can cause injury to the gums and result in their bleeding.
2. It can also cause wear of the tooth structure causing sensitivity of teeth, followed by inability to bite into food.
3. In severe cases, may cause tooth chipping and fracture.
4. Nails harbour bacteria which can get into the body and cause illnesses like stomach infections, flu, and even Tuberculosis (TB).
5. In children wearing braces, the pressure due to nail biting can add to the pressure exerted by the braces and cause damage to the roots of the teeth.

Treatment

1. Wearing of a mouth guard, which can be made in the dentist's office, can prevent the habit and also prevent damage to the teeth and gums.
2. Wearing of gloves can also help to some extent.
3. In less severe conditions, keeping the hands occupied with a stress ball or other objects is advisable
4. In children with psychological problems, an attempt should be made to address these problems first. *This may require consultation with a Child Psychologist.*

6. Lip Sucking or Lip Biting

Thumb sucking or finger sucking habit usually decreases with age, but at times it may get converted into a habit of lip sucking and biting. Thumb sucking habit goes down with age and lip sucking increases with age. Hence, vigil is required to prevent one habit converting into another one. In this habit, the child usually bites the lower lip between the upper and lower front teeth.

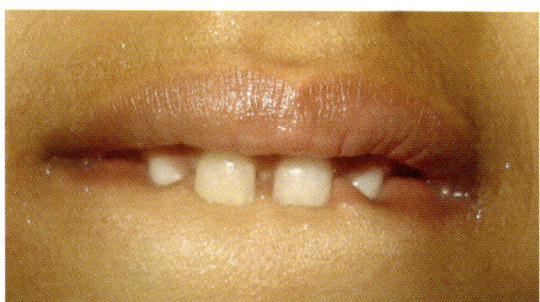

Fig. 7.9 Lip Biting

Harmful effect of lip biting or sucking
1. Dryness and cracking of lips
2. Proclination or protruding upper front teeth
3. Retroclined or retruded lower front teeth
4. Crooked teeth or crowding of teeth

Treatment
1. Use of mouth shields
2. Use of lip bumper (an orthodontic appliance)
3. Use of a mouth guard

I Love to Brush! Routine Dental Care

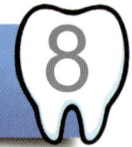

Once the eruption of the primary teeth has begun, care needs to be taken to prevent cavity formation, because we all know that prevention is better than cure. This cannot be more true than in case of dental caries in children. The tooth structure once lost due to dental caries will never regenerate. Sadly, it is lost for life. And I have seen both parents and children cry in my clinic of pain—emotional for some and physical for others. In urban society, dental caries is one of the most prevalent health problems in children. So it is important to set up an oral hygiene regimen for your child from an early age.

Brushing

This is the most effective tool for keeping cavities at bay. The habit of keeping the oral cavity or mouth clean should be started very early, even when the teeth have not erupted. The gum pads should be cleaned with a piece of gauze. Cleaning of teeth should be started as soon as the first tooth erupts. Initially, cleaning should be done with the help of a gauze or a piece of soft and wet cloth. At the age of 18 months, the child should be introduced to the toothbrush. A soft, nylon bristled, small headed, flat toothbrush should be used. The parent or guardian should train the child to clean their teeth twice a day, once in the morning and once at night before going to bed.

Here are some oral hygiene tips which will be helpful not just for the children, but for adults as well.

Types of toothbrush

1. **Manual toothbrush**

    a. Finger toothbrush: It can be slipped over the finger of the parent or guardian and is really convenient to use as the finger has the flexibility to move everywhere in the mouth.

    Fig. 8.1 Finger Toothbrush

    b. Long handle parental care brush: It has a long handle so can be used easily.

    Fig. 8.2 Long Handle Parental Care Brush

    c. Small head toothbrush with a thick handle: This is easy to hold for the child and is another option once the child stars brushing by himself or herself.

    Fig. 8.3 Baby Brush

2. **Motorized toothbrush:**

    These are quite efficient. Children just seem to love this kind of a toothbrush. Some really fancy ones with lights, music and all kinds of cartoon characters are available.

    Fig. 8.4 Motorized Toothbrush

Once the child gains control over hand movements and their dexterity improves, they can be handed the brush so they can start brushing on their own. The child may not be able to do a good job initially, but will be able to manage with a little help from the parents or guardians. Children tend to chew the brush which can cause flaring of the bristles. The toothbrush should be changed if flaring of the bristles is noticed.

Fig. 8.5 Worn Out Tooth Brush

Question: What to do if your child shows lack of inclination for brushing?

1. The child should be motivated to clean the teeth to get rid of bacteria.
2. Education of the child should be done in a playful and interesting manner.
3. Reading stories of the child's favourite characters brushing their teeth can go a long way to help.
4. If your child loves to mimic and copy you, let him or her do so and make brushing a family affair.
5. Let the child observe himself or herself in the mirror while brushing.

Brushing techniques

1. Clean the outer surface of the teeth positioning the toothbrush along the gum line.
2. With a gentle back and forth motion, clean the chewing surface of the teeth.
3. Use the tooth brush at approximately 45 degrees to clean the inner surface of all the teeth.
4. Never forget to brush the tongue as it has a rough surface and harbours maximum bacteria, which may even lead to bad breath.

Fig. 8.6

Flossing

In India, even we, the parents, are not in the habit of flossing our teeth, but it is important that we teach our children to do it. Brushing cannot clean the plaque and food debris wedged between the teeth, which can only be cleaned with the help of dental floss. Flossing should be introduced around the fourth year, so that by the age of nine the child is proficient in using dental floss.

Types of floss

1. Waxed dental floss
2. Unwaxed dental floss

 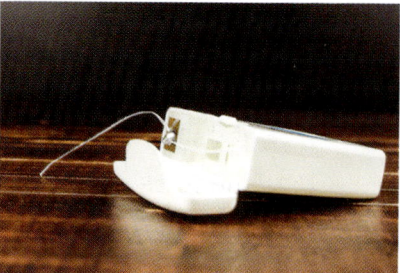

Fig. 8.7 Type of Floss

3. Braided floss
4. Flavoured floss
5. Dental tape
6. Single use mounted dental floss (Superfloss)

Flossing technique

It is not of much importance which floss we use, as they all work well. What is important is that the proper technique is followed.

1. Flossing should be done every day, especially at night.
2. Take about 18 inches of floss and wrap the two ends around the middle finger of both hands.
3. Hold the floss securely between the thumb and index finger of both hands.

Fig. 8.8

4. About one inch of floss that is left between the two hands is softly pushed in between the teeth and is gently worked up and down to clean the space between the teeth.
5. Remove gently either by pulling at one end or by sliding it out.
6. Repeat this process for all the teeth.
7. Care must be observed to prevent injury to the gums.
8. If the child finds it difficult to floss according to this procedure, form a loop by joining the ends of the floss. Hold it between thumb and index finger and use as explained earlier.

Toothpaste

Toothpaste is a tooth dentifrice. When used with a toothbrush it helps in cleaning the teeth and maintaining their gloss. It aids by reducing the surface tension of water, hence easier removal of plaque or tartar from the tooth surface. It leaves the mouth feeling fresh and clean. Toothpastes can be fluoridated (with fluoride) or non-fluoridated (without fluoride). Fluoride goes a long way in fortifying the enamel of the teeth and making them strong and resistant to the attack of acid-producing bacteria which produce cavities.

Fig. 8.9

Protocol for the use of a toothpaste

1. The American Academy of Paediatric Dentistry states that no toothpaste should be used initially, till the age of two years.
2. Toothpaste of the size of a pea is all that should be used at one time by children for brushing.
3. The child should be taught to spit out the toothpaste and not swallow it.
4. Toothpastes, specially made for children, are available. These have low amount of fluoride (up to 500 ppm), as compared to the normal tooth pastes and their use should be encouraged.
5. After six years of age, normal toothpaste may be used.

Benefits of fluoride

Fluoride is largely responsible for the reduction in dental caries. *Fluoride is both safe and effective in preventing and controlling dental caries.* Fluoride is available in toothpastes and mouthwashes, through drinking water fluoridation, and professional application by the dentist in the form of gel and foam. Half-yearly fluoride treatment in the dentist's clinic reportedly caused an average decrease of 26 per cent in caries incidence in the permanent teeth of children. The application time for

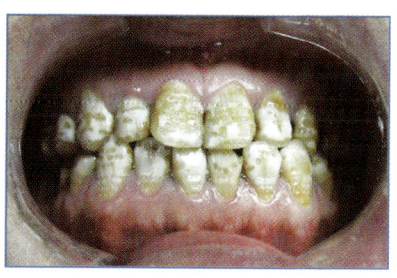

Fig. 8.10 Result of Excessive Flouridation

the treatments is only four minutes in each sitting. The drawback with fluoride is the hypomineralization of the enamel (rough enamel surface) and subsequent brown discolouration of teeth, if not used judiciously.

Fluoride swallowed while brushing, during the age when tooth development is taking place, can also result in a range of visually detectable changes in enamel opacity (that is, light refraction at or below the surface) because of hypomineralization. These changes have been broadly termed as Enamel Fluorosis, certain extremes of which are cosmetically unacceptable [Figure]. *However, a low prevalence of mild enamel fluorosis has been accepted as a reasonable and minor consequence when compared to the substantial protection from dental caries provided by fluoridation of drinking water.*

- **Other cleansing aids**

There are some other products available that help in mechanical or chemical cleansing inside the mouth. These have to be used as an adjunct to the above-mentioned methods to maintain better oral hygiene.

1. Interdental or Interproximal brushes
2. Gum massagers
3. Tongue cleaners
4. Mouth rinses or Mouthwashes
5. Toothpicks
6. Water picks

Dentist—My Best Friend! Regular Visits to the Dentist

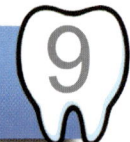

Do you remember when you went to a dental clinic? Probably not! But do you remember *why* you went there? Chances are—toothache! Now, this should not be the reason for your first visit to the dentist. A visit to the dentist should be a regular feature every six months.

The first visit to the dentist is of huge importance. The experience during this visit leaves a lasting impression on your child's immature mind.

It is here that the dentist and the child need to develop a rapport and a friendly relationship. We, as dentists, make sure that this first visit is comfortable and not traumatic to the child.

Therefore, the first visit to the dentist should be as early as one year of age! Often, though, the first visit is not earlier than three to four years of age, that too when the child complains of pain during chewing or due to a swelling of the gums.

The Paediatric Dentist (Paedodontist)

Paediatric dentistry is the specialty of dentistry that focuses on the oral health of young people.

A Paedodontist is the dentist who is trained and specializes in the treatment of oral diseases in Children, though, a General dentist is also equipped to deal with children.

They examine the teeth of your child to check for dental caries, normal and abnormal development patterns, abnormal habits like thumb sucking, finger sucking, nail biting and tongue thrusting, and advise the parent and the child if any corrective treatment is to be done.

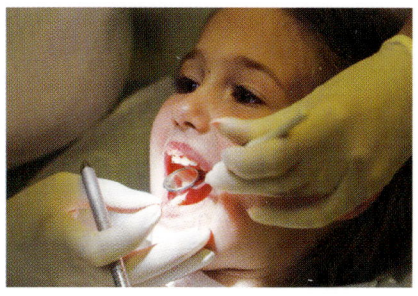

Fig. 9.1 Dentist Examining a Child

Listed below are a few characteristic features that your child's dentist should possess:

a. They should be concerned about your child's total health care in addition to good oral health since oral health is an important part of general health.

b. They should be soft spoken and understand the psychology of the child, in addition to being considerate to the child's special needs.

c. They should be ready to devote adequate time to the child. Patience should be a virtue with any doctor, especially while treating a child patient.

d. They should make sure that the visit to the dentist is a pleasant one so that confidence and trust can be built for a lifetime.

e. They should reinforce the necessity of regular brushing and flossing habit at home.

Pre-visit preparation of the child:

1. Speak to the dentist regarding what will happen at the clinic and explain to the child beforehand. This would make the child less afraid and more cooperative.
2. Never scare the child regarding the visit to the dentist ever. Always portray dentists in a friendly light.
3. Tell the child some pleasant stories of other children's visit to the dentist. You can also read out stories from the many books available on this.
4. Always carry to the dentist the child's medical file with details of any special condition or medication the child might be under.
5. Make sure your child has a good sleep the night before the appointment. Also make sure your child is well fed before meeting the dentist.

Psychology of the Child and Uncooperative Behaviour

Uncooperative behaviour is one complication which both the dentist and the parents are scared of. At this time, it is of utmost importance to understand the psychology of the child. Fear of the unknown is a well-known fact and this is applicable to the child also. The dentist's place is an unknown territory for the child, hence all effort should be made to familiarize him or her with the surroundings, the dentist and assisting staff, the dental equipment, and the procedure to be carried out.

In spite of the best efforts, at times the child may throw tantrums and be extremely uncooperative. In such cases, at times, the dentist may decide to reschedule the appointment. Sometimes multiple visits with the dentist may be required before even the simplest treatment can be carried out.

Management of the child

1. The tell-show-do method is a commonly applied tactic. By taking the child into confidence and explaining before doing the treatment helps in building the child's confidence in the doctor.

2. By talking to the child during examination helps in distracting him or her from the environment and becoming relaxed in the dental chair.

3. Giving an example and showing the child an obedient and cooperative child helps the child patient gain courage and accept treatment better.

4. Praising the child for every small good deed done and rewarding the child for being well-behaved at the end of treatment is another valuable tool.

5. Voice modulation and maintaining a soft but firm tone can help in controlling some uncooperative kids.

6. In a few cases, using nitrous oxide or laughing gas can calm the patient. In extreme conditions where a procedure has to be carried out, general anaesthesia may be required.

First visit to the dentist

1. The first visit to the dentist is usually a short one and usually involves very little treatment.
2. Sometimes the dentist may ask the parent to hold the child in the lap and sometimes may ask them to wait in the waiting room, as the situation demands.
3. The dentist will then examine the teeth of the child to check for dental caries, normal and abnormal development patterns, abnormal habits like thumb sucking, finger sucking, nail biting and tongue thrusting.
4. The dentist will educate the parents and the child regarding daily oral hygiene practices and advise the parent and the child if any treatment is required.
5. Basic cleaning, polishing, and fluoridation procedures may be carried out.

Emergency Visit and Dental Care

Evulsed or fallen out tooth: A condition like this may happen due to trauma. First and foremost, the parent or caretaker should look for the fallen tooth. It should be washed gently with water and, if possible, it should be replaced into the socket. If this is not possible, the tooth should be carried in a clean container of water, cold milk, or saliva. The faster you get to the dentist, the better are the chances of salvaging the tooth.

Cracked or chipped tooth: In case of a chipped or cracked tooth, you must contact your paediatric dentist immediately. Quick action can prevent infections and save the tooth. Gently rinse the chipped tooth with water and apply cold compresses to reduce bleeding and swelling, in case of soft tissue injury. If the broken tooth fragment is found, place it in cold milk or water and bring it to the dentist.

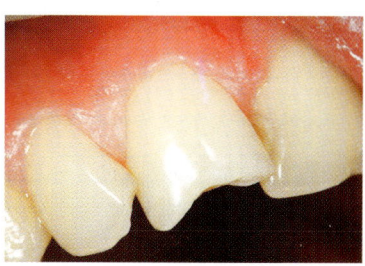

Fig. 9.2 Fractured Tooth

Pain and swelling related to dental caries: In case of pain and swelling due to dental caries, an emergency appointment should be booked with the dentist. In the meanwhile, a common painkiller in paediatric dose should be given to the child after taking advice from the dentist. Rinsing should be done with cold water, but no external application of hot or cold pack should be done.

Fig. 9.3 Tooth Pain and Swelling

Fracture of jaw bone: This is a condition which warrants hospital visit and treatment. It should also be kept in mind that a blow to the head can be life-threatening and should not be taken lightly.

Beautiful Smile Orthodontics for Your Child

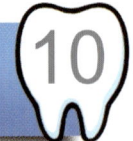

Orthodontics is the branch of dentistry which deals with prevention, interception, and correction of problems related with the alignment of teeth, that is, crooked teeth. In today's times, this is a very important part of dental treatment. Everyone wants to look beautiful and attractive, for which a good smile is essential.

Preventive and Interceptive Orthodontics

This part of orthodontics deals with the education and motivation of the parents and the child regarding the normal and abnormal growth pattern and prevention of abnormal development.

Conditions which need attention and correction in children from 6 to 11 year of age include:

1. Premature loss of milk teeth
2. Retained milk teeth
3. Permanent teeth erupting in an abnormal position
4. Supernumerary teeth or extra teeth
5. Abnormal growth patterns of the face
6. Habits like thumb sucking, mouth breathing, lip biting, etc.

We shall discuss these factors one by one.

Premature loss of milk teeth

Loss of milk teeth well before their shedding time occurs mainly due to dental caries and sometimes due to trauma or accident. We have discussed prevention and treatment of decayed milk teeth in earlier chapters. Here we shall elaborate on what can be done when such a situation arises. There are certain options available in these cases.

Space Maintainer: Early loss of a back tooth (molars) can cause the teeth adjacent to it to move into the empty space. Hence, the space which was meant for the permanent tooth becomes smaller or even closed. As a consequence, the permanent tooth erupts is an abnormal position and crowding of the permanent teeth occurs. This problem can be prevented by the use of an appliance called a space maintainer.

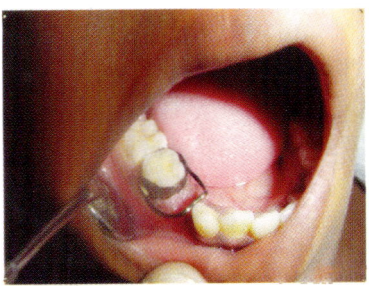

Fig. 10.1 Space Maintainer

As the name suggests, this device maintains the space created by the loss of a deciduous or milk tooth till the permanent tooth starts to come out into its position. This appliance can be either removable or fixed. A fixed appliance is preferable as the child cannot take it out and a better result is thus achieved.

Space Regainer: As the name suggests, this device helps by re-creating the lost space to enable the permanent tooth to erupt in its proper position. In children where the space has already closed after tooth loss as no space maintainer was given, now an appliance called a space regainer is given. This, again, can be removable or fixed.

Replacement of front tooth: There are psychological effects on the child due to the loss of the front teeth. The child may become conscious of their looks and retreat within themselves. They may also develop complexes because of other children teasing them. It can also cause a change in their speech. So it is of utmost importance that the tooth is replaced with an artificial tooth.

Retained milk teeth

It is frequently seen that the milk tooth has not fallen but the permanent tooth starts to erupt. This needs immediate attention as you need to show the child to the dentist. This milk tooth, which can be mobile or loose, needs to be extracted immediately to prevent the permanent tooth from coming out at the wrong place.

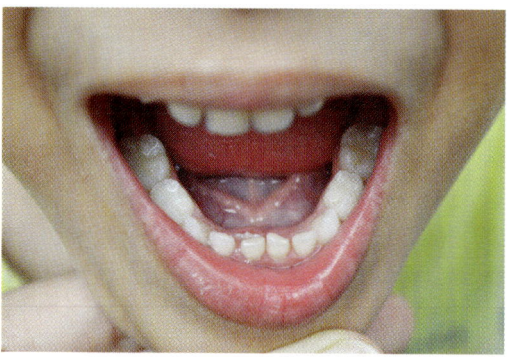

Fig. 10.2 Milk Tooth Not Fallen, Permanent Tooth Coming Out

Permanent teeth erupting in an abnormal position

At times, even with no apparent cause, the permanent teeth tend to come out in a place other than where they are supposed to be. A very common example is the canine tooth erupting in the gum above the space meant for its eruption. In such children, an appliance should be given to bring the tooth into its correct space.

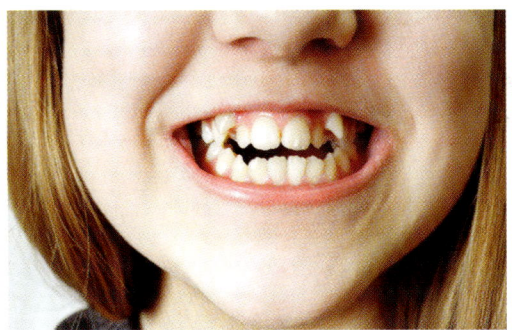

Fig. 10.3 Canines Coming in Wrong Position

Supernumerary teeth or extra teeth

Between the two front teeth, in very few children, a sharp small tooth is seen. This is an extra tooth and is called a supernumerary tooth. This tooth creates space between the upper central incisors, hence causing their displacement. This tooth needs to be removed, followed by an appliance to close this space.

Abnormal growth pattern of the face

You may have observed that in some children have an abnormal face profile. In some, the lower jaw looks underdeveloped and in some children the lower jaw is too prominent. All these cases need the appropriate appliances to correct the situation. Hence a visit to the dentist, at the earliest, is advisable. The best time to start treatment in these cases is from 7–10 years of age. However, the dentist may initiate some intermediate treatment earlier, if required. This decreases the intensity of the developing problem, easier treatment, and better result later on.

Habits

This is the most important part of preventive and interceptive treatment and, keeping this in mind, I have dedicated a whole chapter (We Call them Bad Habits) to this cause.

Abnormal Looking but Self Correcting Condition

Ugly duckling stage: This condition is seen related to the eruption of the permanent canines. The pressure exerted by the erupting canine on the roots of the permanent incisor causes these teeth to look flared or fanning out. But this condition does not need treatment as the subsequent eruption of the canines into the mouth will cause the teeth to come into normal position.

Corrective Orthodontics

Once the milk teeth have fallen and the permanent teeth have erupted, which is usually around 11–14 years of age, we can be sure that this is how the teeth will finally be. The child can now be assessed if orthodontic treatment is required, whether for aesthetic reasons or for functional reasons. Both removable and fixed appliances can be given to the patient, depending on the type and severity of the problem. The removable appliance is commonly called plate and the fixed appliance is called braces. In both treatments, the trick is to move the teeth into correct position by putting pressure on them, as this results in tooth movement.

Conditions needing orthodontic treatment

1. Irregular teeth, crooked teeth, or crowding of teeth
2. Protruding teeth or teeth coming out
3. Spaces between teeth
4. Improper positioning of teeth.

Braces are used to correct these cases. Braces are the most effective and predictive way of treating patients. They provide the dentist maximum control on the tooth movement and patient compliance is better. The treatment time with braces is usually two years,

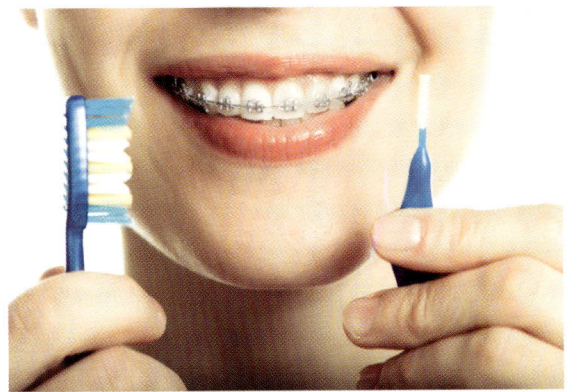

Fig. 10.4

plus or minus six months. Sometimes, in the course of treatment, it might be important to remove some teeth. There is nothing to worry about this as the space automatically closes with treatment. Braces can be of metal or they can be of ceramic or transparent material.

Care to be taken with braces

1. Proper brushing and brushing after every meal is important so that food does not remain in the mouth as this can cause both gum problem and cavity formation.
2. Care should be taken that you do not bite using the front teeth. All fruits and finger foods should be cut with a knife into small pieces and chewed using the back teeth.
3. You should avoid all sticky and sugary foods to prevent cavities and discolouration around the braces.
4. Do not put pencils and pens into the mouth as it may loosen and distort the braces and wires.
5. Retainers must be worn after treatment, as advised by the orthodontist, to prevent relapse of treatment, as the teeth have a tendency to return to their original position.

Spaces between deciduous teeth are good (and not a problem) because the permanent teeth which will erupt in their place later will be bigger in size and will need more space to grow properly. This will reduce the chances of crooked teeth and malalignment.

Braces

Braces are used to move the teeth into their correct position. That is, to correct the aesthetics and also the functioning of the teeth, jaws, and muscles. The treatment can take from six months to two years—or even more—depending on the severity of the problem. Conventional braces consist of the following parts:

1. The brackets, which are glued on to the teeth, and which hold the wire in place.
2. The wire, which is engaged into the brackets, to move teeth along a desired path.
3. The modules, which hold the wire in the brackets.
4. Sometimes elastics are used to apply pressure on the teeth.

Different kinds of braces are available today, namely:

1. Metal braces
2. Ceramic (tooth-coloured braces)
3. Metal self-ligating braces
4. Ceramic self-ligating braces
5. Lingual braces
6. Aligners

Metal Braces

These are the traditional braces which are metallic in appearance. They are least expensive but they work well. The drawback is the appearance—looks like a mouthful of metal.

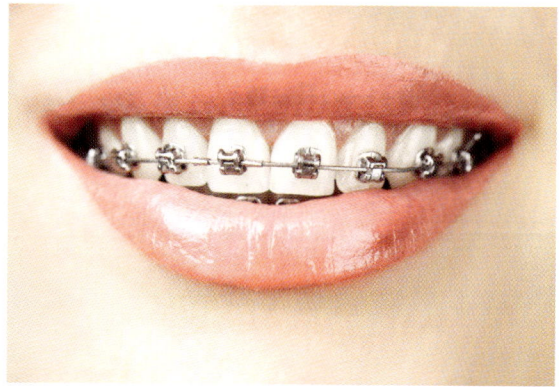

Fig. 10.5

Ceramic Braces

They are tooth coloured hence have better aesthetics. They blend with the teeth, so are ideal for the appearance conscious. They need to be taken care of as they stain easily. They are relatively more expensive.

Metal Self-ligating

The braces are metallic in appearance but hold the wire in the brackets on its own. No modules are needed in this system. There is less resistance and therefore requires lesser time for the treatment. Another benefit of these braces is that pain during treatment is substantially less because the teeth are relatively free to move in the bracket as they are not bound by the modules.

Ceramic Self-ligating

These are tooth coloured brackets and hold the wire in the bracket on their own. The other benefits are same as metal self-ligating.

Lingual Braces

These braces are glued to the inner side of the teeth, hence, are not easily visible. They are of great use for models and people conscious when dealing with public. These are not really recommended for children. They can cause difficulty in speech and cannot be used in people with small or narrow jaws.

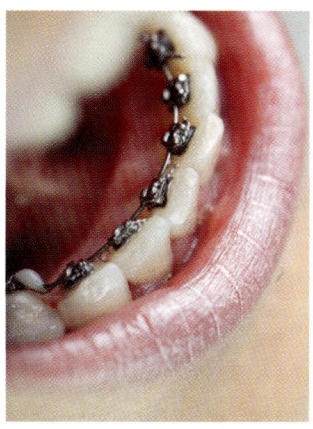

Fig. 10.6

Aligners

They are popularly known as "invisible braces" and, correctly so, as they are barely noticeable. They consist of a set of about 18–20 mouthguard-like appliances, which are worn by the patient in a sequential manner, one after the other. The first aligner is replaced by the next appliance every two-three weeks. Usually, the dentist decides when you are ready for the next set.

The biggest advantage is that they can be worn to work without people noticing anything readily. So a lot of adults prefer this over the conventional braces. These aligners are also slightly less troublesome in the initial stages, and cause negligible bruising in the mouth.

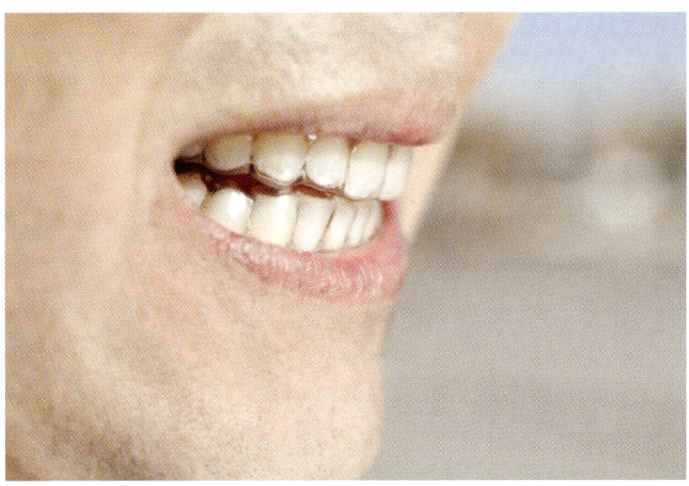

Fig. 10.7

There are a few limitations in this mode of treatment. They may not be as effective in cases where the teeth show severe crowding (overlapping of teeth). They are removable by the patient, so the patient may not wear as regularly as is advised, which would increase the treatment time. The cost of treatment is also much higher.

More Blessed or Less Children with Special Needs

The need for routine home care, regular check-ups, and familiarity with the team providing dental care is of utmost importance for children with special needs.

Fig. 11.1

Routine care habits at home keep the child's teeth in good condition. Three to six monthly check-up by the Dentist is important to identify the problem in the incipient stage. Familiarity with the Dentist goes a long way in creating a home-like comfortable and trusting bond between the child and the Dentist, which makes it easy for the child to undergo treatment, when required.

Listed here are some dental findings in children with special needs.

1. *Tooth development*
    - Eruption of teeth may be delayed, accelerated, or inconsistent.
    - Before teeth eruption, the gums may be swollen or bluish-purple in colour.

2. *Crooked teeth*
    - The upper and lower teeth may not bite well into one another.
    - Crowding of teeth may be seen.

3. *Tooth anomalies*
    - Pits, line, or discolouration may be seen on the tooth surface.
    - Tooth shape, size, or number may be different.

4. *Incidence of tooth decay*
    - Crooked teeth are difficult to clean hence more susceptible to decay.
    - Malformed development of the outer layer (enamel) allows decay to start easily.
    - Sugar contained in medication makes teeth more prone to cavities.

5. *Accidental trauma*
    - More frequent in children with intellectual disability, seizures, lack of muscle coordination and those physically challenged.

6. *Gum problems*

Early and severe gum problems can be seen due to:
    - Inadequate oral hygiene

- Impaired immune system
- Medicines like Phenytoin (for seizures), Calcium channel blocker (for blood pressure), and Cyclosporins (immunosuppressants) can cause swollen gums which can lead to difficulty in chewing, bad breath, and poor appearance.

Routine Home Care

The method of routine oral care is the same for all; what is important is how to achieve it.

Brushing twice a day

To get the child interested in following your brushing instructions, ask him or her to show you how to brush and, in a playful way, give your inputs on the brushing method.

Using a Fluoridated toothpaste

This is very important. Most of the kids tend to swallow toothpaste, so use limited amount of toothpaste—it should cover only half of the toothbrush.

Brushing technique

The care giver should themselves learn proper brushing and flossing from the Dentist.

Electronic toothbrush

Use of electronic tooth brush for children who have poor manual dexterity can be helpful.

Consistency

Consistency of technique, place, and timing is important.

Mouthwash

Use of Chlorhexidine mouthwash regularly is another good habit. If the child finds it difficult to rinse, then a chlorhexidine spray is equally effective.

Dietary Habits

1. Avoid using sweets, colas, etc., which can cause cavities, as rewards and incentives to the child for their achievements.
2. Rinsing with water after taking medication containing sugar will keep the child's teeth safe.
3. Children with xerostomia (less saliva in the mouth) should be asked to drink water at short intervals. Keeping a sipper handy is a good idea.
4. Children on medications which cause swelling of gums should be taken to the Dentist for frequent check-ups. They may require cleaning of teeth (scaling).
5. Professional fluoridation and pit and fissure sealants are highly recommended.

Trauma

In case of an accidental injury, follow this procedure:

1. If the tooth has fallen out of the mouth, pick up the tooth and put it in milk or water immediately. Rush to the Dentist with the child. This tooth, at times, can be fixed back into the mouth, with some further treatment. If this is done within 30 minutes, the same tooth can stay successfully in its original place.

2. If the tooth is loose but still in the gums, rush to the Dentist for putting it back in the proper position.

Visit to the Dentist

1. The first visit to the Dentist should be done definitely before the child's first birthday.
2. A couple of visits for familiarity with the dentist and the environment are important for a smooth and successful dental treatment.
3. Take care *not* to scare the child or show any signs of fear in the presence of the child.

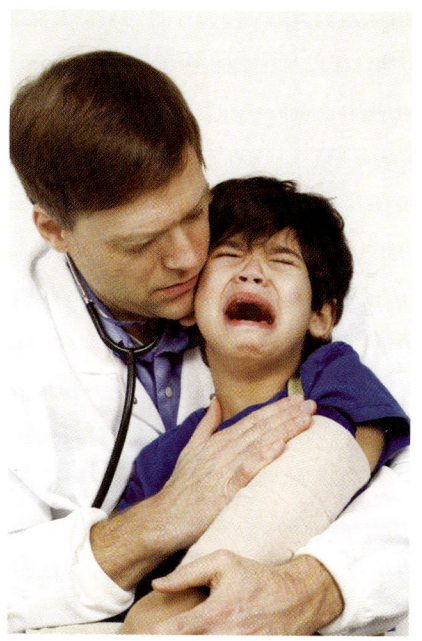

Fig. 11.2

4. Let the child be rested and in a good mood before the dental appointment.
5. If child is not comfortable or cooperative in spite of all the efforts in the right direction, ask your Dentist about sedation.
6. If everything else fails, the option of general anaesthesia can be discussed with the Dental Surgeon.

Inculcating the right oral hygiene values in children with special needs may require patience, perseverance, and a lot of time. It can take more effort on the part of the child, the parents and the Dentist, but it will have a positive bearing on the child's dental and general health. This would definitely improve the quality of life for the parents as well as for the apple of their eyes.